not locked up anymore

A collection of poems from past and present situations that will free any church member, family member, or friend from any kind of circumstances you have battled in your life but never knew how to release them.

angela williams

Copyright © 2015 by Angela Williams

All rights reserved. No part of this publication may be reproduced, stored in a retrieval system, or transmitted in any form or by any means, electronic, mechanical, recording or otherwise, without the prior, written permission of the publisher.

Published by:
Godly Writes Publishing
P. O. Box 2005
Orangeburg SC 29116-2005

Free — Not Locked Up Anymore
ISBN 10: 0970409346
ISBN 13: 978-0-9704093-4-8

Cover design by Greg Jackson, ThinkPen Design

10 9 8 7 6 5 4 3 2 1

For Worldwide Distribution, Printed in the U.S.A.

acknowledgements

I would like to thank God for making this poetry book a reality. You brought me through tough love and situations that helped me become stronger and mature in the Word. I love You and praise You for everything I encountered over the years, for I learned that in everything, to give You thanks.

I also want to thank the family of the late Rev. Dr. H. T. Williams for embracing me in my youth and letting me be a part of their family while I was growing up. Mama Williams and the children were always there for me. Rev. Williams taught me the Word of God as my first pastor at St. Paul Baptist Church in Orangeburg, South Carolina.

Thank you to the late Bishop Jack. F. Koger for being a great father to me and teaching me the principles of the Bible. Memories of his love and encouragement will always remain with me. To his wife, Rev. Dr. Betty C. Koger, thank you for letting me work under you for 25 years at Grace and Truth Christian Center and giving me the knowledge and understanding of the Word, so I could preach the truth of the gospel without fear. You have helped me reach depths in my life as well as conquer fears of moving forward toward what God has called me to do.

To my sisters, Vivian, Frances, Marshalette, and my brothers, James, Earl, and Scott, thank you. I would not be satisfied if I had been born into another family. You have been there for me through thick and thin. We had hard times, but we stuck together and made it.
To my aunts and uncles, Patricia Johnson, Mary L. Bonaparte, Annie Williams, Heyward Bonaparte, and Rev. Nathaniel Bonaparte, my mother's siblings, thank you for pushing me forward in life. Even when I didn't quite make it, you were always there to help me and encourage me. My nieces and nephews, especially Olivia, Rolanda, Shay, Deandre, Davin, David, Tammie, Audra, LaQuinta, Bridgette, and all my cousins, you are special in my life. I love you Judith Johnson, Joyce Johnson and Regina Johnson, Jacqueline Corley and Valarie Caffey: my girls I raised.

To all my other families, the Walls, Snellings, Battles, Darbys, Griffins, Seawrights, Carmichaels, Brooks, Wylies, Clarks, Rices, W. A. Perry Middle School family, and some other great people in my life, I salute you. To the best sisters and brothers adopted in my family, Rose Corley, Roy Green, Connie J. Piper, Leroy Smith, Josiland W. Jackson, Stephanie B. Boyd, and my new sisters, Cynthia Jackson and Janice Wylie, I say I love you and thank you. You were always there for me and with me, giving advice, praying for me, and sharing with me. Words can't express my love for you. You all have made quite an impression on my life, and I will always cherish it. Thank You.

You are the BEST!

dedication

This book of poetry is dedicated in memory of my mother, the late Mrs. Lillie M. Bonaparte Reed, who passed away in 2007. She was the inspiration behind such an expressive way to write poetry.

She was always kind and quiet about things she dealt with in her own life. No matter what people said about her or how they treated her, she never retaliated or spoke unkind words back to them. She had a way of letting go that I didn't understand until she was gone from the earth. Her meekness taught me many lessons on how to handle my own situations without being rude or disrespectful.

I decided, one day while watching my mother fight her own health battles that I needed to release my experiences through writing. I've been through family issues, mistreatment with church folks, friendship problems, and other seasons in my life that God has delivered me from. I didn't know how I would get through it all, but I always had my mother's words. I am free to be me in any setting today, and it was not an easy task. I fought long and hard to gain my own sense of direction and victory over every battle in my own personal encounter with people.

I always remembered what my mother taught me that "the battle is the Lord's, not mine." I am grateful to have had my mother's powerful influence in my life, for it made the difference and made me who I am today. She's not here, but I can still hear her say, "I am so proud of you, ANGIE."

This book is also dedicated to the late Mrs. Elizabeth A. Battle, my other "mama" who came into my life when I was 15-years-old. She nurtured me, protected me, provided for me, and gave me some of the best times of my life. I will never forget the late night conversations, the discipline, and the love shown toward me from the Battle and Snelling families.

Ma Battle is what I called her. Her Christian life spilled over into mine, and I was taught the Word of God and how to really pray through her life and examples. Our lives were meant to collide so that I could get on the right track and become who God called me to be. She was there when I got licensed, ordained, went off to college, and got my first home. She will always be remembered. I truly miss you and love you.

table of contents

Foreword	x
Introduction	xv

Part 1: Skeletons Out The Closet

Encounter of Another Kind	19
It Happened Again	20
Listening To The Other Voice	21
Comfortable In Your Skin	22
Help! I Think Too Much	23
I Stand Accused	24
Back And Forth	25
Trusting Leaders	26
Can I Be Real?	27
Lying Again	28
The New Preacher	29
Time To Leave	30
2nd Time Around	31
What Happened To The Message?	32
Guilty By Association	33
A Hired Hand	34
Snapping Under The Pressure	35
I Found It In The Church	36

Part 2: Think You Can Remember?

Sister, Sister	39
Free To Be Me	40
Didn't Take The Time	41

Get Up And Get Behind The Wheel	42
Whatever It Takes	43
Getting	44
The Crooked Road	45
The EBT Card	46
A Straight Line	47

Part 3: Family Love

Dedicated To Mother	51
Dual Roles	52
The Day She Died	54
Grieving Without Pain	55
I Am Healed	56
The Walls	58
She	59
But She Did It Anyway!	60

Part 4: Days of Our Lives

I Did It!	65
Where Are The Children?	67
Coming Home...	68
Incarcerated	69
He "ain't" The One	70
Sleeping With The Enemy	71
Noisy People	72
If The Truth Be Told...	73
Saved, But Rebellious	74
Let It Go	75
Get That Monkey Off My Back	76

Part 5: Seasons

Seasons	79
Christmas	80
Christmas II	81
Keep Your House Clean	82
In Your Care	83

Part 6: The Real Truth

The Truth	87
The Unchurched Church	88
Moving Beyond	89
I Choose You	90
He's More Than Music	92
If Walls Could Talk...	93
The Cross I Bear	94
Who Is God?	95
By The Way	96
Can It Get Better?	97
B'cauz	98
Peace	99
A-l-o-n-e	100
A Call From The Altar	103
About The Author	105

foreword

Encouraging. Spiritual. Inspirational. These are the adjectives that come to mind when I think of *Free —Not Locked Up Anymore*. These are also words to describe the attributes of Angela.

She was one of the first to welcome me to a new school as a teacher and to become a part of the W. A. Perry family. Throughout the years that I have known Angela, she has always been the same. She has always been kind, loving, caring, funny, encouraging, spiritual, and inspiring. I met her when I was employed as an English Language Arts teacher, and we had the relationship of simply co-workers. Later, we grew to become friends and as close as family.

As I read Angela's book of poetry, I released tears of joy and hope, and I let out the sound of laughter. Angela's compassion for people and her love for God and life are definitely evident in her works; she has a heart of gold. All that Angela has experienced throughout her life has produced the works of this book.

I can definitely relate to "Sister, Sister." Just as it had been difficult for Angela to be bound by struggles of life regardless of her many gifts and abilities, I, too, have faced the same struggles. "Didn't Take Time" especially brought tears to my eyes because it is so often that I forget to acknowledge how awesome God is because I get so caught-up into the distractions of life. Angela's poetry encouraged me to listen to God's voice more than my own.

"In Your Care," another one of my favorites, reminded me of Christ's love, on-going, never-ending presence and my salvation because of Him, which should never be taken for granted. *Free — Not Locked Up Anymore* also displays Angela's love and dedication for her family, her students and especially, her mother. Another favorite of mine, "Who Is God," was so enjoyable for me that I wanted to read more.

Regardless if you're a saint or a sinner, regardless if you're a child or an adult, regardless if you know God or if you've never known Him at all, if you've ever felt depressed and lonely, discouraged and abused, disappointed, frustrated, hurt by your sister, your brother, your friend, your pastor, your wife, your husband, or anyone at all, read *Free — Not Locked Up Anymore*. The one main reason why you should read *Free — Not Locked Up Anymore* is to help you to know yourself. These poems, more than anything, will encourage you to be free. Free to find out who you really are and free to be who God has ordained you to be. *Free — Not Locked Up Anymore* will spiritually encourage and inspire you to be free to be you.

—Celeste Goings

introduction

This collection of poems is based on real life experiences from the author in everyday situations. This book will deliver and set you free from ordeals you have encountered at home, in your family, in the church, in organizations, in marriage, and in other relationships.

Have you ever been through anything and can't seem to shake free? Read this book and be set free from people, places, and things. I was able to extricate myself from people, from places that left a bad taste in my mouth, and from things that I had put ahead of God.

The hardest part of deliverance is forgiveness. Through writing these poems, I have been able to forgive family, friends, churches, pastors, ministers, leaders, teachers, colleagues, and, most of all, myself. It is a blessing to wake up every morning happy and free. I purpose to never be in that kind of bondage again.

Like any other person, I dreamed of the good life and never thought I would deal with so much drama. I learned that "the prayers of the righteous man availeth much." Someone somewhere was praying for my deliverance, and I received it. Thank God for delivering me and setting me free.

Jeremiah 29:11 reads, "God has a plan for my life which includes a future and an expected end." I can't wait to see what God has next for me!

part I
skeletons out the closet

encounter of another kind

Today, I had to do something odd,
It involved people I loved, so it was hard.
But I know if I don't, they'll never make it,
And in the end, I don't think I can take it.
I poured my heart out, not knowing what's next.
It wasn't about alcohol, drugs, or sex.
I told the truth so help me God,
I can go back down the path I trod.
It was an encounter of another kind,
It dispels myths and straightens some minds.
I hope that what I shared wasn't in vain,
'Cause the battle for lives is victory's gain.
It's worth it when someone's life is spared,
The devil doesn't like you, so don't even dare.
Give him an inch, and he'll take your smile,
And cause you pain for a long, long while.
So get away from not doing God's will,
Let the enemy see you can't be still.
You'll have encounters that may not feel good,
But in the end, you'll be glad that you stood.
For when you think your day is just fine,
You'll have an encounter of another kind.

it happened again

I got molested again last night,
while my family was fast asleep.
I wondered why it kept happening to me
I guess it's because I'm called the "black sheep."
He made me be quiet and tried to penetrate,
I lifted and moved, and he missed the place.
I can't really tell you whether it hurt,
I hide my feelings and the dirt.
One day I will be released of this crime,
The horror— the hurt that runs through my mind.
I didn't deserve to be violated and used,
But it was safer to please people and get abused
Well I told my mother, but she didn't dare,
For fear that the family would be mad and stare.
And accuse us of being so lame and so weak,
We were more than poor, just very bleak.
Each day I awaken, I thank God for life
I had to forgive, get rid of the strife.
God gave me the grace to write it all down,
And now I'm free, I CAN STILL WEAR A CROWN.

listening to the other voice

You were born to be something,
I heard the Lord's voice
But still ringing in my ear
Was another man's choice.
I tried so hard to get up and do
What You called me for, but couldn't get thru
Everywhere I turned, there was pain and stress
My life, my decisions, and choices— a mess.
I've come to the conclusion, it's You alone
No matter who knocks or calls on the phone
Listening to the other voice was not so good
It made me miss out on doing the things I should.
I have no peace, no joy down inside
My life's spinning around like I'm on a joyless ride
Maybe if I changed and quieted my voice
Listening to the New Man might be a good choice.

comfortable in your skin

Are you walking 'round in derision,
Trying to make a wise decision.
Just look in the mirror at the condition you're in,
You caused it, get comfortable in your skin.

Be yourself and not another,
God made you different from any other.
You don't have to retaliate or set up a friend,
Just be comfortable in your skin.

Laugh, have fun, say how you feel,
The other one of you is not for real.
The pleasure of life comes if you win
Get excited and comfortable in your skin.

You're not a model or a defender,
You don't even have to be a pretender.
Things can go straight in the end,
If you can be comfortable in your skin.

help! i think too much

Help! I think too much
I gather my thoughts and begin to clutch
Wondering how people do what they do
To make your life hard the way they do.

Help! You know I think too much
Paying my way as I choose to go Dutch
Saying in my heart what I hear all the time
Reflections of crazy things controlling my mind.

Help! Is there a cure for this?
Or should I just stop and make a list?
Of the promises of God found in the book
I think I'll stand in the mirror and take a good look.

My mind needs to be renewed
The thoughts running round need to be reviewed
The ones that cause me great sickness and pain
Shall no longer be used for profit and gain.
HELP! I Think Too Much

i stand accused

I went through Hell today,
Got accused of people falling away.
Didn't do it, though they said I did,
Another lie slipped into Satan's bid.
Anger and tears were pressing me so,
The enemy then became my new foe.
It's confusing when you can't think right,
You make a lot of mistakes 'cause you're so uptight.
You answer the thoughts running 'round in your head,
Sometimes you even wish you were dead.
Then they couldn't accuse you no more,
Of the people that walked right out of the door.
These people hadn't planned to live for the Lord,
They hated the sermons preached from the Word.
They just make excuses to get you in trouble,
The book of James talks about minds being doubled.
I stand accused, but freed by His grace
I was found not guilty— I rest my case.

back and forth

I've been down this road before,
Vacillating between yes or no.
Can't make up my mind, no matter how easy,
My stomach's in knots, I'm feeling kind of queasy.
If I could just say what's on my mind,
My life would be better; I'd be doing fine.
But fear has me in this divisive grip,
So I just look all around and seal my lip.
I desire to talk and tell what I know;
It's much more peaceful going with the flow.
Back and forth down the road of pride,
Many times failing and trying to hide.
If I renew my mind and look ahead,
Back would be my past, forward I would be led.
For destiny's calling me to move on up,
To give me purpose, please fill my cup.
I don't have to live the way that I do,
I buried back and forth, and upward I choose.

trusting leaders

Honey, can I trust what you have said?
I'm not the only one with the gossip you've fed.
It seems like preaching the gospel is a game,
Everyone just wants its honor and fame.
God left you in charge to preach the Word,
To those who will listen— who haven't heard.
You have the right to live clean, pure, and holy,
So others can see the beauty of God's glory.
Let your light shine around the dark places,
Instead of lying, stealing, and pretending faces.
You better get it right and become trusting
Before hell is your home 'cause you keep on lusting.
People are looking for leaders to trust,
Moral character and honesty are a must.
To help someone as they pass your way,
Trusting leaders are what we want TODAY!

can i be real?

Can I be real with the truth about you—
How you change, lie, and gossip, too?
Can I be real about the price I paid
To cover up your messes, a mistake I made?
If walls could talk, all would discover
You're a fraud with a good heart to uncover.
Crooks get caught, but you slip away
By the year, the month, each and every day
Can I be real and tell what I know,
So my life can go on, like a friend, not a foe?

lying again

She did it again, lied through her teeth
Denying all charges above and beneath.
Uninhibited and crazy consequences
False advertisement on the fences.
People believing all the time
Everything spoken at the drop of a dime.
Cell phone, low key, voice in silence
Promoting hearsay, gossip, and violence.
Can you tell me why the stuff's not stopped?
There's scripture that says it should be dropped!!!

the new preacher

A new preacher just came to our church
Arrogant and pushy, looking for self-worth.
Finding fault, criticizing from bottom to top
Seeing issues with everbody, the faithful crop.
He is heavy, high-minded, and never feels wrong
About talking nasty, being rebellious and strong
His attitude won't change because of his past
Brought into his new life, a history to last.
The flame of deceit and gossip burns on and on
Don't know how long, one day he'll be gone
Until he realizes the damage he's mangled
The pain in innocent eyes, the knife he's dangled
Cutting out joy and laughter when present
Making remarks not called for, not so pleasant
He'll always be remembered as the preacher who could
But never made progress for God, like he should.

time to leave

Several years gone by—
It's time to leave.
But you're still holding on
Friendships to cleave.
You'll never become
All that you can be
Until the past is released
And you run toward Me.
I told you to get up
And say your goodbyes.
But you stayed even longer
With tears in your eyes.
Trying to please everyone
Instead of pleasing Me
It was your time to leave—
Almost missed your destiny

2nd time around

This time is almost like the last
Full of hypocritical blasts.
Same old story different folks
Lying, tricking, making jokes.

Told the leaders some new lie
Added extras so the scheme would fly.
Trying to discredit me so much
Like a broken ride without a clutch.

Couldn't believe they've been taken again
Same old tricks from the father of sin.
Listening to garbage from a member at large
Like a bullet trying to be dodged.

Can't keep doing the same old thing
Getting ridiculed for my believing.
Don't understand the life of a fraud
Help me! Please, help me Lord!

Dreamt about who the culprit was
Saw how they schemed without a cause.
But it won't last cause it aint true
Soon be over, my victory due.

what happened to the message?

What happened to the message
You are supposed to be preaching?
Throwing out feelings of flesh
To the ones you should be reaching.
Months gone by, you haven't read much
Words from the pulpit, never heard such.
Hard to reach others when you lose your cool;
Can't talk too much, you're acting a fool.
Used to be good at what you do best—
Preaching, teaching, passing all your tests.
What happened to the message from the One on high?
Those do-it-yourself sermons just don't fly.

guilty by association

Many things I did not do
But guilty by association.
Accused and sentenced by the few
Not the entire congregation.

Didn't always know what went down
Said I'd probably be the one accused.
Tied up, tangle, gagged and bound
Frustrating and hurt from being misused.

This can't keep on happening
Time to move to another place.
Got to get myself back on key
Not guilty any more— I rest my case.

a hired hand

Called to preach the gospel
By the Lord and not by man.
You followed what people said
And became a hired hand.

Don't preach about sin issues
Or the wrong the members do.
Can't talk about bad attitudes
Might have a nasty one, too.

Go out your way to pretend
To have the people at heart.
You only want their money
To make you a fresh start.

Got ideas how to scam
With stories from the world.
Been practicing all your life
From different ones you've heard.

When you try to reach the masses
Give the gospel plan to man.
Or are you going to keep living
The life of a hired hand?

snapping under the pressure

When the shoe is on the other foot, it matters not.
When the shoe fits your feet, things get very hot.

You snap at many people and still call it love,
But the attitude behind it can't come from above.

It's okay when you say things that you believe,
But when truth comes forth, your heart won't receive.

We've had our hard times and now yours has come.
Will you snap under pressure like a man being hung?

Go get your mind together and see truth as it is;
Let God help you through and get your case dismissed.

i found it in the church

Looking for hate
Wanting to fight,
See the whoremongers
Crooks out of sight.

Looking for war
On the choir stand,
Ushers on the wall
Exchanging their man.

Looking for sorrow
From the saved pulpit,
Smoking, hot preachers
Can't wait to get lit.

If you don't find it
Anywhere else,
Stop by the church
It's on everybody's shelf.

Whatever you need
To get you off track,
You can find it in church
And that's a real fact.

part 2
think you can remember?

sister, sister

Sister, sister, sitting in that chair,
Full of good ideas, but no one to care.
Wanting to fulfill your passionate dream,
Of being a great teacher, and leader it seems.

Sister, sister, get your thoughts right
Don't give up because of the fright.
Can't share with others whose job is to steal,
Rip you apart, destroy you, your future to kill.

Sister, sister, why drop your head?
You know the plan, by God be led
Tell the truth no matter whom you hurt
Get the monkey off your back, get rid of the dirt.

Sister, sister, fit into the will of God
And walk down the road, the path others trod
Complete the call of God on your life,
Let go of anything that brings you strife.

Sister, sister, your work's almost done
You've stood the test, a race almost won.
Bless your heart for the progress made,
You're a good sister, I see the path you've laid.

free to be me

Free to wake up every morning
And lift my hand;
Free to walk and talk
And take a stand.

Free to sing and worship
And praise the Lord;
Free to hear the Word
And be on one accord.

Jesus paid the ultimate price
That I might have eternal life.
He gave His life on Calvary's cross
To save His people that's sick, diseased, and lost.

Free to be me is not a burden;
It's a decision and a choice.
You can receive it any time
By speaking and using your voice.

Just ask the Lord to give you the Word;
Free to be me, free to be heard.
Make up your mind to give Him the praise;
Free to be me, free songs to raise.

didn't take the time

Woke up this morning feeling blessed,
Had many night dreams, but not much rest.
Set out to give the Lord some praise,
Rushed right through the day without a phrase.
Can't figure out why things are so tough,
Bills, house, school, gas and stuff.
Maybe I can step right back in line,
Lift my hands up and connect to the vine.

Didn't take the time to let the Lord know,
How I appreciate His gentle, kind flow.
Of the Spirit of life that wakes me each day,
So I can start it off right, take time to pray.
I can't forget what He has done for me,
Gave me joy, peace, and victory.
So no matter what happens from this day on,
I will give Him the praise 'til my work is done.

get up and get behind the wheel

you were headed somewhere
before the accident;
you still have a job to do
you're the one He sent.

no one can handle the road
like what flows out of you;
the speaking power of God
full of Spirit and Truth.

push past the experience—
the hurt and the pain;
many souls will come forward
from the strength you proclaim.

get ready for your destiny
by any means necessary;
you will never be defeated
by Satan, the adversary.

whatever it takes

Whatever it takes,
I'm gonna get it right.
Whatever it takes,
I'm gonna win this fight.
Whatever it takes,
I'm gonna do my best.
Whatever it takes,
I purpose to pass this test.
Whatever it takes,
I'm going to finish.
The race set before me,
Without defeat or diminish.

getting

Church is <u>getting</u> to be good,
Just like I knew it would.
Takes time to get the people right,
Praising the Lord is out of sight.

Church is <u>getting</u> to be sound,
Healing the sick, loosing the bound.
Scriptures telling how to live,
Malachi 3 telling how to give.

Church is <u>getting</u> to be great,
People on time and not being late.
Purpose and plan coming together,
Taking care of God's business despite the weather.

Church is <u>getting</u> to be in demand,
Voices rising all over the land.
Gas prices up, everything so high,
Cause His return draweth nigh.

the crooked road

I went down a path;
Thought it was straight.
Found out it cost more,
Than today's going rate.
Kept going on, trying to find,
Someone to share my lies with.
Was not as hard as I thought,
Simple people fell for the myth.
I've been down this path before,
The same thorns and thistles there.
Time to find my real self-esteem,
And get off the crooked road that's bare.

the ebt card

The EBT card came one day
To buy food for the fridge at bay.
It started out as an innocent look,
But I kept getting tempted to become a crook.
Bought groceries and then took them home;
Some of the products ended up gone.
No one knew what was going on—
Kept lying, secrets shared over the phone.
Suppose to be a saint, but a crook I am;
Don't care who knows, not even the man.
Figured I wouldn't get caught so soon,
But the Father above saw me, now I'm doomed.

a straight line

A straight line looks like a heart with no beat,
A student in class who gave up his seat.
It can be a good thing if you're walking around,
But not a great path if you want to stay down.

A quest for answers to a hard decision,
No curves, no humps, just a point on a mission.
Trying to see where things tapered off,
Whether in baseball, football, skiing or golf.

You can find a straight line when walking upright,
A direction to a destiny when traveling by light.
A leveling plane when retracing a line,
A breath of fresh air, a pattern by design.

part 3
family love

dedicated to mother

Just watching you lie
Quietly in your bed.
Nodding out several times
While shaking your head.

Reminds me of some things,
You taught me when I was small.
To depend on the Saviour,
Problems large or small.
We learned a Bible verse
At the table we'd quote.
Where it was found
Written by hands on a note.

You said that your father
Did the same thing for you.
Made sure you knew Jesus,
Like he knew Him, too.

So I say thank you
For all you have done.
I've got a path to now follow
I have victory already won.

dual roles

In memory of
Lillie Reed and Marilyn Jamison

Out of different worlds,
Emerged two beautiful women.
Not having so much in common,
But they both knew the word, amen.

Marilyn was a nutritionist
Sis. Lillie an aid to a teacher.
Telling everyone about Jesus
Was the top of their double feature.

They both laughed and ate well
Cleaning the entire plate.
One getting her early sleep
The other staying up late.

The one thing they both did
Was attend the same church.
Working hard to learn more
Using the Bible to do their search.

Sis. Lillie had great wisdom,
And Marilyn had the young age,
But the results of their dual roles
Put the church on center stage.

If we could turn things around,
We'd invite them to come back,
But the course that they just finished
Didn't have room for any slack.

So we're proud to have had Marilyn
And Sis. Lillie on our team.
Their spirits still encouraging us
To do well and fulfill the dream.

the day she died

Lost my mother to death today—
Full of pain, words just can't say.
The tears wouldn't fall, so much to do
A wake, a funeral, the weeks after, too.
Found myself full of questions, so lost—
Couldn't eat or read, nor bear my cross.
I got out my Bible and the scriptures read
Tossing and turning while lying in bed.
Trying to understand what happened so quick
Breathing, heart beating, now gone in a flick.
The day she died didn't surprise me at all;
I had been reading the written up wall.
I believed the words of the prophet so true;
Now I can get through the aftermath, too.

grieving without pain

I started out hurting deep within;
No, I had not doubted, nor did I sin.
I walked around, but not in depression;
Not knowing what lurked in my mind's obsession.
Went to the Lord and poured out my heart,
Needed love, joy, and peace— a brand new start.
What others said couldn't take away the pain;
The voice in my head would never complain.
All of a sudden, my pain went away;
Good memories and dreams kept coming each day.
Even though I'm grieving today without pain
Trusting in the Savior is strength beyond strain.

i am healed

I went to see the doctor,
And he said I had cancer.
Of all the things I ever desired,
This sickness was not the answer.

It attacked my body hard,
Made everything seem to hurt.
For the shell I actually live in
Was created from pure dirt.

The medicine worked off and on,
Giving me a very false feel.
So I pleaded the blood of Jesus,
Thank God, I am healed.

The pain's still there in reality,
But the Word of God is greater.
Not by evil force of the enemy,
I'm healed by truth, not a traitor.

I am healed, I am healed,
No matter how the situation looks.
My faith, my trust, and confidence,
Is found in the Bible, the great book.

I left you for a little while,
But soon, you'll see me again.
Through faith taught in my church,
My running was not in vain.

the walls

The Walls are a family on fire;
They've been with me and kept me alive.
Feeding, lodging, and sharing their things,
Praying, loving, and listening to me sing.
They gave me something I never knew,
True friendship and love all the way through.
Over the years, they pulled me in close,
Covering my faults like cheese on toast.
I can't express how grateful I am,
To have such friends when I'm in a jam.
The measure of love they give of themselves,
Can't be found in a book or on any shelves.
They added me to their family tree,
"Prodigal daughter," mama Wall said, that's me.
I tried to keep in touch with their lives,
Clinging to relationships like sharp knives.
Meditating, reminiscing, how they blessed me so,
By always being there for me with a glow.
"Good to see you" is always what I would hear,
The Walls have been friends year after year.

I salute Dad Hoover, the late Mama MaryAnn,
Annette, Shane, and Hattie. You are truly family.

she

She came to the church
As a willing and giving vessel,
With the Word of God tucked
In her spirit, quite nestled.
Speaking boldly with full knowledge,
Laughing and having fun with the members.
Sharing what she had learned in school,
Full of wisdom and an awesome helper.
She imparted good ideas and thoughts
As she went along life's journey.
Mother, daughter, sister, and friend
Frankly, her name was Marilyn, you see.

but she did it anyway!

This is a very hard day in my life
I trust God to get me through it

It's not easy to fathom a very sick parent slipping away. It's difficult even more when your latter years of relationship drew you closer together. I think about and constantly recall all the laughter, fun crazy ideas, and joy she has brought into my life. The day she called to say I'm not coming to church still echoes in my head. I can see her being upset about missing church. She was always there even in days of pain and agony. She's been there for all of her children and given her time, energy, love, food, and money at the risk of losing her own,
But She Did It Anyway.

She rode the city bus and shared the gospel with everyone she could. Sometimes she would get up in church and say things. Some people sneered, others whispered and even though others insulted her feelings and said mean things under their breath,
But She Did It Anyway.

She ate foods she couldn't have any longer, stood on those legs and cooked day and night for the family, catered for programs on her job, stayed after school to help others in spite of being over tired. Walked long miles even when it hurt so bad,
But She Did It Anyway.

Whether hurt, insulted, talked about or lied on, she showed the love of God. Whether destroyed by people's ways and how they handled her, laughing, picking, talking down to her, she still loved them. When there shouldn't have been any love left to give the people, she still found some love somewhere to give,
But She Did It Anyway.

Now it's her turn to have love returned, but she's not able. She doesn't recognize her people, family, or church members. Her life is calling for change, a plan of salvation to those who knows her. She wasn't supposed to be incoherent and sick like this. She wasn't supposed to leave us wondering, staggering, and sad,
But She Did It Anyway.

Many times she did it anyway. Just to show the love of Christ, not perfect, yet forgiven by God, and able to forgive all of us regardless to what the issue was, she did it anyway. She left a legacy that will forever be here. Look at her now. Gone to eternity when we told her to stay here. She Did It Anyway.
We love you, Mama!

part 4
days of our lives

i did it!

From the creation of earth
To the day of your birth—
I did it.
The crying, the laughter, the pain,
The weight of your gain—
I did it.
Letting you run loose and free
Voicing your opinions of me
I did it.
Walking by your side
Helping, even when you lied—
I did it.
Schools, careers, jobs, and more
weeping, cleaning, mopping the floor—
I did it.
And when your work is finally done
You'll hear my voice say, "Well done."
Because in all you went through
Family, friends, and good times, too—
I did it.

where are the children?

Where are the children
born in this sinful state,
conditions of lust and temptation
running off their plate?

having good times, going to parties,
late night chats and deals.
power struggle over territory,
bullets flying around our heals.

oozies, magnums, reefer, & smoke,
can't even tell which one's mine.
setting myself up for a wasted life,
planning on tips and dropping a dime.

how do we find our children
in the midst of this heavy rage?
tight clothes, makeup, and body motions
dramatic, confused, mind not engaged.

God, what did we do to them
when we stopped being the head?
ruin them, hurt them, marred them
now they're almost all dead.

coming home...

Got a call from the fed
Then one from the pen,
A desire to come home
Just don't know when.

A knock on the door
With a quick silent grin,
The answer was "Yes."
I could come home again.

I packed my boxes and bags
And sold all the rest,
Got a ticket to ride the bus
Front, maybe backseat I guess.

Telling family was a nice treat
Not sure the pain and questions I'd hear.
Confusion, envy, hate or love
My past emotions I fear.

Coming home, getting closer
To destiny for my life.
Said I would change, but not true
Brought home the same old strife.

Shared old times from the past
Skeletons up from the grave.
Back on the block, same old thing
Know I should be saved.

Lord, I want to come home
But really not like this.
A new life, a clean heart
On heaven's saintly list.

incarcerated
incarcerated
incarcerated

Started out as a dream one day,
Then life's reality hit.
Got locked up and shook down,
Then sent to the prisoner's pit.
Got some new friends,
Giving out insane advice.
Why I keep listening,
He already paid the price.
Now my mind's messed up
From the people with no God.
Could have walked away at anytime
But I just sat there and nod.
So incarcerated in my mind
In another whole new way.
Just can't wait to get released
Before I crack up today.

he "ain't" the one

Yo' man ain't no good at all,
Not by your bedside nor on call.
Bringing women in and out yo' home,
Sinning like you're already gone.
Won't answer the phone or the cell,
Deeds he's doing will send him to hell.

Thought he loved you, guess I was wrong.
My heart is hurting, for I knew all along
He wasn't the right one from the start,
Just had a good job and played the part.
He forgot he'll reap whatever he sows,
The lies and falsehood, so many whores.

Can't get mad, not even angry with him,
You taught me better, let the Word condemn.
When it's all over, and life moves on,
You'll see your life under the sun;
Get rid of your fake dreams and run.
Wake up girl, he ain't the one.

sleeping with the enemy

By the way, his name is Chuck
I married him, and now I'm stuck.
Went on a date, and he paid my way
Now I can't get him to work a day.

Won't cut the lawn or wash the car,
Just want to look at things from afar.
Putting movies and games above the Lord
Been a long time since we've been on one accord.

Pretending to be a Christian at church
Fighting, cussing— I'm on a new search.
Sleeping with the enemy didn't happen by chance
I thought it was love— a brand new romance.

If I had known it would turn out like this,
No vows would have been said, not even a kiss.
Lord, help me to put the pieces all back
From sleeping with the enemy and his vicious attacks.

noisy people

Noisy people, making noisy praise
Run and shout all over the place.
Giving honor and plenty of laughter
From the floor to the top of the rafter.

Challenging spirits to get up and flee,
Bringing the saints true victory.
Noisy people, bad and so bold,
Spirits subjected, brought under control.

Needs being met all over the church,
Bodies getting up from beneath the earth.
Tell me what noisy people won't do,
Stand up, be counted, the next one's you.

Noisy people, making noisy praise,
Run and shout all over the place.
Giving honor and plenty of laughter
From the floor to the top of the rafter.

if the truth be told...

Used to watch you from the pane
Strutting and flashing in the other lane.
Took her husband right in her face
From the choir, usher board, and any other place.

Used to watch you play bingo— hard
Cheating and lying with just a nod.
Fishing and dipping in other men's matters
Telephone gossipping and unfriendly chatters.

Cussing and smoking under the tree
On the church grounds smoking weed.
Didn't make a difference if your life was unfold
You just don't care if the truth be told.

saved, but rebellious

You would think that all is well,
But the church is still going to hell.
Saying what they just won't do,
Living a life different from the truth.

Coming on Sunday to all the events,
Asking good questions with great pretense.
Won't work a job or pay a bill;
Just plain stubborn, against God's will.

Keep on mumbling under your breath;
Confusion keeps bringing mounds of debt.
Told you to watch what you say;
Killing yourself day by day.

So saved, yet rebellious are you;
An outright sinner, so nasty and rude.
Can't tell anyone what's right these days;
Better give up and change your ways.

let it go

I cried again last night
Deep in sorrow and woe,
But I heard a voice from within
Saying, "Quiet, child. Let it go."

Let go of the past with its sadness;
Remember the good times of gladness.
Walk away from the shadows of fear;
Leave the old days that gave no cheer.

Where you used to face hurts and pain,
And the people who used you for gain:
Let go of whatever makes you hate
Before you die in sin, and it's too late.

Let go of the evil thoughts to get even—
The power of failure that kept you in sin.
Pride, jealousy, animosity and strife
Will zap all your energy and destroy your life.

So let it go, the pain of the past
Of abuses, the other offences won't last.
Pick up the pieces of your broken-ness, too;
Only Jesus can put you together anew.

get that monkey off my back

Got that monkey off my back,
gossiping, lying— on the wrong track.
Bout' to get myself in trouble,
jumped out the mess on the double.
Done this so much, it's so stale,
leaving a bad record to trail.
Can't help it, gotta know what's down
so nosey, so moody, without a frown.
Should be trying to lead the way,
but I like news from day to day.
The only way to keep up with things,
bad marriages, funerals, and personal flings.
Why can't I just tell the truth,
doesn't matter to me, there's no proof.
Getting away with dirt for years,
phone calls, visits, laughs, and cheers.
Gonna catch up with me someday,
the love and respect will be washed away.
Could have lived a better life, you see
so I could spend my time in Eternity.

part 5
seasons

Seasons

Seasons have changed;
My life is rearranged.
Things are out of control;
Your hand I long to hold.

It used to be warm;
No hurt or no harm,
Quiet nights, starry skies
Now just sobs and cries.

The pain grows stronger;
The days get longer.
The seasons have changed;
My life feels strange.

Got a new outlook
From the powerful book.
In the midst of the season
I have my pure reason.

Show me which way, Lord
So my seasons are on one accord.
Breezes of your fresh spirit
changed my life, now I can bear it.

christmas

Christmas—
Cold weather,
Music playing,
Stores very busy,
Children sleighing.

Still not the same
As that day of old
When Jesus came down,
And the story unfolds.

He came as a babe
In a manger one day.
There was no other place
For Him to stay.

I'm so glad it happened
Don't know what I'd do.
If the plan of salvation
Wasn't offered to me, too.

christmas ii

Christmas means giving back
Of your time and yourself
To the Christ who came
Lived, died, and left.

To make sure you can have
Eternal life forever
Praising, giving, and living
True peace and joy never ending— forever.

This is why Christmas Day
Should be spent with all our friends
Remembering Jesus loves us so much
Showing His love to the end.

keep your house clean

Just because they visit you
And buy you little things.
Just because they call the cell
With three or four loud rings
Don't mean you let your guard down
And eyesight no longer keen.
Stay in the Word of God,
And keep your house clean.

Don't be fooled by flattery of words
And the glitter that doesn't really shine.
The loud music, the catchy smile
From your friends, their friends, and mine.
Put on the whole armor of God
And meditate like a well-oiled machine.
Focus on the Will of the Father,
And keep your house clean.

I'm not talking 'bout the fleshly heart
That pumps the blood right through.
But the Spirit man on the inside
That can see the real, true you.
False ways, mean looks, lies on stage
Sin from the wrong kind of genes.
Don't get caught up in yourself,
But keep your house clean.

in your care

Waking up,
Looking around,
Saying thank you,
Without a frown—
I was in Your care.

Making choices,
Setting goals,
Feeling down,
Sweats and colds—
I was in Your care.

Tell you the truth
From the beginning,
All through life
And every inning—
I was in Your care.

Thank you for all you've done;
Making life great for me.
Blessings sent from heaven
Giving me victory—
I was in Your care.

part 6
the real truth

the truth

Tonight at church, we heard the truth—
Sin-filled lives must be uproot.
No nods of heads, no yeahs and sighs—
A cold silence of grief, pain, and denial.
Can't help but think what can be done
To bring about change through the Son.
People heard what was said but refused
To turn it around, stop being used.
By the devil and his imps pushing hard;
Just say amen to truth and dump his card.
I'm so excited about the revelation
Of righteousness, cleansing, and salvation!
It's good to know that the truth will tell
How we must know Jesus so we won't go to hell.

the unchurched church

While preaching the Word in the church downstairs,
sex and illicit drugs, happening in the balcony chairs
staying away from the words that bring change,
filling the church with people so strange.
seduction and roots taking hold by large,
hypocrites and liars— thieves in façade.
rap music in place of the gospel so long
feels right to keep doing exactly what's wrong.
letting young people live like they want to
jailbirds, homosexuals, lesbians, the crew.
gotta put a stop to this dangerous living,
make the church understand the things God's giving
the life we're living is not pleasing today;
must get to know Jesus in the right way.
salvation and power can be given to all
if you would only just answer the call.

moving beyond

I've seen the lightning flash;
I've heard the thunder roll.
I've seen the results of sin
    taking over my soul.

I've cried out to the Lord,
Wondering just how long
I'll go through this turmoil,
Because I chose the wrong.

I guess things won't change
Until I do something different.
Like give my life to Christ,
In his word my time well spent.

Now I know what I missed
Deep down on the inside.
A clean heart and pure mind
Where only Christ abides.

i choose you

Before the foundations of the world,
I chose you.
To go preach and teach the Word—
I chose you.
You haven't prayed or read your Word,
My voice you just haven't heard.
You're walking around in your flesh
When only I can give you the best.
But still yet, with all your shortcomings—
I chose you.
You took my money, and you lied.
You failed because you didn't try.
You talked and caused so much division,
But now it's time to make a decision.
If you only reach out to discover—
I chose you.
Not because you could pray
Or sing and shout all day;
Not because you could attend
The very best of everything;
Not because of your goodness
Or because of your nastiness,

But because I came and died
I was hated and crucified,
So that you could make it in
If you could pray and understand—
I chose you.

I chose you...

he's more than music

He's more than music
dancing in your head;
or words from your vocal cords
and notes that you just read.

He's more than music
or thoughts you entertain;
jumping with the choir
your living now in vain.

Don't try to figure Him out
just flow with the beat;
tune in to the salvation plan
stay away from the heat.

Let your heart be saturated
with the blood of Jesus Christ,
and you'll know He's more than music
when He comes into your life.

if walls could talk...

From birth to earth,
I'm on the scene.
Eating and crying,
All smart and keen.

Asking questions like crazy—
Pushing for facts.
How did I get here?
Hey! By what kind of acts?

If walls could talk,
They'll tell the story.
How we made many mistakes
And not all for His glory.

We professed to be Christians—
Something we're not.
Hoping that everyone
Would have soon forgot.

But we have to stop,
And face the life we've messed up,
And ask God for forgiveness
Receiving love and mercy in our cup.

the cross i bear

The cross I bear has been quite a chore:
Making decisions, walking through a strange door.
Talking about new challenges to face,
Crying, fighting, tears all over the place.

"How could this happen to me? " I asked.
I have a full load, don't need another task.
I've learned to respond in a positive way,
Put God in charge of my full scheduled day.

The cross I bear no longer seems too hard,
Not handling the problems myself is really odd.
Breathing easy at every step I now take,
Asking for directions with all the moves I make.

who is God?

He's my day-breaker,
My only way maker.

My bridge over troubled water,
My outstanding lawyer.

My way, truth, and life,
My success in the midst of strife.

My favor in the sight of man,
My blueprint on the page of His plan.

The blessed great "I AM,"
The comforter for my "fam."

The teacher of my knowledge,
The financier for my college.

The future driver of my ride
When from the earth I leave this side.

by the way

By the way, did you thank Him?
Did you remember what He had done?
How He gave His life on Calvary—
The love of His only begotten Son.

By the way, what will you do
When all is at risk and you're lost?
Will you reflect on Christ's love
And the blood shed to cover the cost?

He paid a debt He didn't owe
He gave Himself to set you free.
By the way, did you know
It was for all as you can see?

By the way, my praise has grown
To a daily increase of His power;
Lifting Him higher, saying thank you
And staying in His presence every hour.

By the way, have you found
To help you through the day
His sufficient grace abounds
When you can't find your way?

can it get better?

Can it get any better
In your life today
Than having your sins
Purely washed away?

Can it get any better
Walking in divine health
Having all provisions
Like a person of wealth?

Can it get any better
When friends talk about you
'Cause they don't understand
God's power you choose?

Can it get any better
So many houses and land
To be blessed and so gifted
You're the center of His plan?

b'cauz

Because of Who You are
Lord, I adore you thus far.
Because of how You died
In my life You will abide.

You came and gave Your life
Made a great big sacrifice
You're now my best friend
Down to the very end—
It's all because of who You are!

Because of when You came
I will always praise Your name.
Because of what You shared
You gave me ultimate care.

You bless me with Your love
Sent down from heaven above.
From way down within
You took away my sin.
It's all because of who You are!

peace

Quiet times,
No noise at all
No worry or problems,
Struggles or toil—
Just peace.
Moving forward
Heaven in view
Made a quality decision
Body and mind brand new
Just peace.
Nothing missing
Nothing broken
The blood of Jesus
A great token
Just peace.
Peace is a thing
We need most definitely
Only Christ can give it
Poured out so infinitely
Just peace, just peace, just peace.

a-l-o-n-e

I was with my leaders and my friends
Having much fun, laughing 'til no end.
Talking and sharing all about my day
My work, choices were not easy to say.
I gave them a run down on what I did
But the loneliness felt, I kept and hid.
I felt no one really understood me
And what I was going through.
They had their own problems
Didn't share or talk them out, too.
Why tell them what's on my mind
And then give them more
To talk behind my back
When I exited the door?
It grieved me to know you can be in a crowd
And still be lonely, no matter how loud.
I decided to talk to the Lord instead
I shared at night as I lay in my bed.
God gave me an answer and showed me favor
My life would be different with a change in behavior.
And now I'm not lonely, not lonely anymore
My new Friend, the Spirit, just walked through the door.
That I left open to the enemy by mistake
And closed the chapter on loneliness, now I'm awake.

a call from the altar

Our Father, all those who have read this book, I bring them and their needs before You now. You are Jehovah Jireh, our Provider. We expect from You, by faith, knowing that You will meet our needs according to Your riches in the very glory of Your presence.

My Lord Jesus, said, "All that the Father giveth me shall come to me; and him that cometh to me I will in no wise cast out." (John 6:37)

Dear Father, as these who have read Understanding bring You their praise, prayer and supplication, I know you will answer them according to Your most holy, just and righteous will.

All these things I ask and pray in the name of my Lord and Savior, Jesus Christ! Father, because I know that You will answer my prayer, I thank You in the name of Jesus Christ!

Oh Lord our God, for all of these and other blessings: we glorify, honor, praise, thank, bless, worship, adore, extol, exalt, magnify and celebrate YOU in the name of Jesus Christ! According to YOUR will, it is done in Jesus' name!

If you are a sinner, please pray the following prayer and receive Jesus Christ into your life this very moment. He's waiting for you.

Father God, I come before you now in the name of Jesus Christ. I confess that I am a sinner and I want to be saved from my sins. I do not want to continue in this life of sin. Jesus Christ is Your Son and He died for my sins. Father, You raised Him from the dead!

Jesus, I want You! I really need YOU right now and forever! I invite You into my heart right now. I accept You into my heart right now. Come in and live in me now!

I believe that You have come into my heart and life!

Father, all these things I have asked and prayed in the name of Jesus Christ! Thank You for these and all other blessings! I will live for You and You alone! In Jesus Christ's name I pray, Amen!

I AM SAVED!

dr. angela williams

Dr. Angela Williams was born in Orangeburg, S.C., daughter of the late Mrs. Lillie Reed and the late Mr. Herman Smalls. She is the second oldest of seven children. She attended the public schools in Orangeburg and graduated from Orangeburg-Wilkinson High School in 1977.

Angela furthered her education at Orangeburg-Calhoun Technical College and Voorhees College. She later graduated cum laude from Benedict College in 1995 with a bachelor of science degree in business administration. In 1997, Dr. Williams graduated from Columbia International University with a master of arts degree in elementary education. She has also received her Ed. S degree in administration from Cambridge College.

She received her bachelor of Biblical studies from the International School of Religion.

Angela also received her masters and doctor of divinity from the Spirit of Truth Institute in Richmond, Virginia. Dr. Williams received her doctor of philosophy and Christian education degree from the Institute of Christian Works in Seattle, Washington. Dr. Williams is a licensed and ordained minister of the gospel and has been preaching since August, 1986.

Dr. Williams is now the pastor and founder of Rejoice Christian Center, Inc. Church in Columbia, South Carolina, where she is the pastor. The church is new and is growing rapidly. She is following the purpose of God for her life and expects to see the church move forward as many souls are saved, healed, and set free. The church's motto is "the church where joy is unlimited."

www.ingramcontent.com/pod-product-compliance
Lightning Source LLC
Chambersburg PA
CBHW052028290426
44112CB00014B/2419